BASIC / NOT BORING
SOCIAL STUDIES SKILLS

ECONOMICS

Grades 6–8+

Inventive Exercises to Sharpen
Skills and Raise Achievement

Series Concept & Development
by Imogene Forte & Marjorie Frank
Exercises by Marjorie Frank

Incentive Publications, Inc.
Nashville, Tennessee

About the cover:
Bound resist, or tie dye, is the most ancient known method of fabric surface design. The brilliance of the basic tie dye design on this cover reflects the possibilities that emerge from the mastery of basic skills.

Illustrated by Kathleen Bullock
Cover art by Mary Patricia Deprez, dba Tye Dye Mary®
Cover design by Marta Drayton, Joe Shibley, and W. Paul Nance
Edited by Jean K. Signor

ISBN 0-86530-550-1

PRINTED IN THE UNITED STATES OF AMERICA
www.incentivepublications.com

TABLE OF CONTENTS

CELEBRATE BASIC SOCIAL STUDIES SKILLS

Basic does not mean boring! There certainly is nothing dull about . . .

    . . . finding out whether a cash cow really has any money

    . . . getting to know your way around a dollar bill

    . . . tracking down the nation's gold supply

    . . . showing off that you know the difference between the DJIA, FTC, FDIC, FRS, GNP, and GDP

    . . . figuring out how much money can be made from different jobs

    . . . getting a look inside the places that make millions of coins and trillions of dollars

    . . . playing games with credit (when you don't have to make the payments!)

The idea of celebrating the basics is just what it sounds like—enjoying and getting good at knowing all about money and the workings of economies in the U.S. and around the world. Each page invites learners to try a high-interest, appealing exercise that will sharpen or review one specific economics content knowledge and skill. This is not just another ordinary fill-in-the-blanks way to learn. These exercises are fun and surprising. Students will do the useful work of practicing social studies skills while they enjoy quirky characters who lead them to explore money-related concepts. They'll examine the ways the economy works, from inside their personal piggy bank to the economic markets of the world.

I calculate that economic know-how is just good sense!

The pages in this book can be used in many ways:
- for individual students to sharpen a particular skill
- with a small group needing to relearn or strengthen a skill
- as an instructional tool for teaching a skill to any size group
- by students working on their own
- by students working under the direction of an adult

Each page may be used to introduce a new skill, to reinforce a skill, or even to assess a student's performance of a skill. And, there's more than just the great student activities! You will also find an appendix of resources helpful for students and teachers—including a ready-to-use test for assessing economics skills.

The pages are written with the assumption that an adult will be available to assist the student with their learning and practice. Also, students will need access to social studies resources such as a social studies textbook, almanacs, Internet reference sources, Internet websites, and encyclopedias.

As your students take on the challenges of these adventures with economics, they will grow. As you watch them check off the basic social studies skills they've strengthened, you can celebrate with them!

The Skills Test (pages 56–59)

    Use the skills test as a pretest and/or a post-test. This will help you check the students' mastery of basic social studies skills in the area of economics, and prepare them for success on tests of standards, instructional goals, or other individual achievement.

SKILLS CHECKLIST FOR ECONOMICS

✔	SKILL	PAGE(S)
	Show understanding of and use a variety of economic terms and concepts	10–13, 50
	Recognize how coins are produced in the U.S.	14–15
	Recognize how paper money is produced in the U.S.; identify features on paper money bills	16–17
	Show understanding of concepts and processes related to earning money; identify ways people earn money in an economy	18
	Distinguish between employees and employers, consumers and producers, wages and salaries, needs and wants	18–19
	Show understanding of concepts and processes related to spending money; recognize ways people spend money in an economy	19
	Show understanding of terms and conditions of employment in different jobs	20–21
	Use information about jobs to determine income and make choices about jobs	20–21
	Show understanding of concepts and processes related to banking	22–27
	Use bank account information to explore transactions in a savings account	24–25
	Use bank account information to explore transactions in a checking account	26–27
	Show understanding of concepts and processes related to credit and debt	28–31
	Show understanding of how interest is paid or gained in loaning or investing money; calculate interest	30–31
	Show understanding of budgeting; make a budget	32–33
	Show understanding of the concept of scarcity as a factor in economic choice	32–37
	Identify different economic choices; practice making economic choices	34–37, 42–43
	Show understanding that economic choices have costs and benefits; identify costs and benefits of different economic choices	34–37
	Show understanding of the basic workings of a market economy	38–39, 46–47
	Recognize economic conditions such as inflation, recession, depression, unemployment	38–39
	Distinguish among different types of economic systems	38–39
	Show understanding of the relationships between supply, demand, prices, and production	40–41
	Show understanding of the effects of competition on prices and services	40–41
	Identify incentives for economic choices	42–43
	Show understandings of taxation and uses of taxes	44–45
	Recognize the role of institutions in economic systems (banks, Federal Reserve, governments, etc.)	46–47
	Understand and define a nation's GDP, GDP, exchange rate, balance of trade, and balance of payments	47
	Show understanding of some basic concepts of the global economy	48–49
	Relate daily events to economic concepts	50

ECONOMICS
Skills Exercises

WOULD YOU..? COULD YOU..?

Would you invest in a "cash cow"? Could you put a gold standard in a piggy bank?
Think carefully about each question. Apply your knowledge of money matters.
Then, answer **yes** or **no.**

Mr. Bigg de Posit
BANKER

_____ 1. Would you find robots at **the Fed**?

_____ 2. Could you melt an **ingot**?

_____ 3. Would it be a good idea to **default** on a **mortgage**?

_____ 4. Could you keep a **bond** in an envelope?

_____ 5. Would you advise someone to **invest** in a **cash cow**?

_____ 6. Could someone **mint** a $100 bill?

_____ 7. Would you find ridges on a **milled coin**?

_____ 8. Could you put a **gold standard** in a piggy bank?

_____ 9. Would you find rubber in a **bounced check**?

Can I keep my cash in your bank?

_____ 10. Could you put an **endorsement** on a check?

_____ 11. Would you expect a **nonprofit organization** to pay **taxes**?

_____ 12. Could someone use a camel as a **medium of exchange**?

_____ 13. Would you take a **promissory note** from a scoundrel?

_____ 14. Could you spend money that is out of **circulation**?

_____ 15. Would you expect a **stockholder** to be happy with a **bear market**?

_____ 16. Could you keep silver dollars in a **check register**?

_____ 17. Would you keep a **certificate of stock** in a **portfolio**?

_____ 18. Could you collect **currency** in different **denominations**?

Use with page 11.

Name _____

Think carefully about each question. Apply your knowledge of money matters.
Then, answer *yes* or *no.*

_____ 19. Could you share a **share** of **stock**?

_____ 20. Would you expect to pay **interest** on a **loan**?

_____ 21. Could you buy lunch with **greenbacks**?

_____ 22. Would you hold a picnic at a **clearinghouse**?

_____ 23. Could you use a **debit card** if you had no bank accounts?

_____ 24. Would you be happy to receive **dividends**?

_____ 25. Could you pay an electric bill with a **money order**?

_____ 26. Would you keep rare plants in a **safe deposit box**?

_____ 27. Could you count on the **IRS** to insure your **savings account**?

_____ 28. Would you expect **stock prices** to go up in a **bull market**?

_____ 29. Could you type a **PIN** into an **ATM**?

_____ 30. Would you be happy if someone gave you **blue chip stocks**?

_____ 31. Could you open a savings account at **NASDAQ**?

_____ 32. Would you be able to sit in an office of your nation's **GDP**?

_____ 33. Could you make a **donation** to a **charity**?

_____ 34. Could you get personal financial advice from **Dow Jones**?

_____ 35. Would you shop for wallpaper at the **stock market**?

_____ 36. Could you buy a dinner with **pounds**?

_____ 37. Would you find security guards at **Fort Knox**?

_____ 38. Could you find a foreign language phrase on **U.S. money**?

_____ 39. Would you expect to take a **risk** with an **investment**?

_____ 40. Could you find paper in a **U.S. dollar bill**?

Patricia Proffit
ACCOUNTANT

Use with page 10.

Name _____

WHERE'S THE GOLD?

(And Other Economic Dilemmas)

Penny Wise gives economic advice on the radio. Show off your economic know-how by helping her answer these tricky questions. Offer your answers to such dilemmas as what to do with an entrepreneur, where to find a teller, and remembering whose faces are on dollar bills. Choose one or more answers for each question. Choose answers that are reasonable or likely.

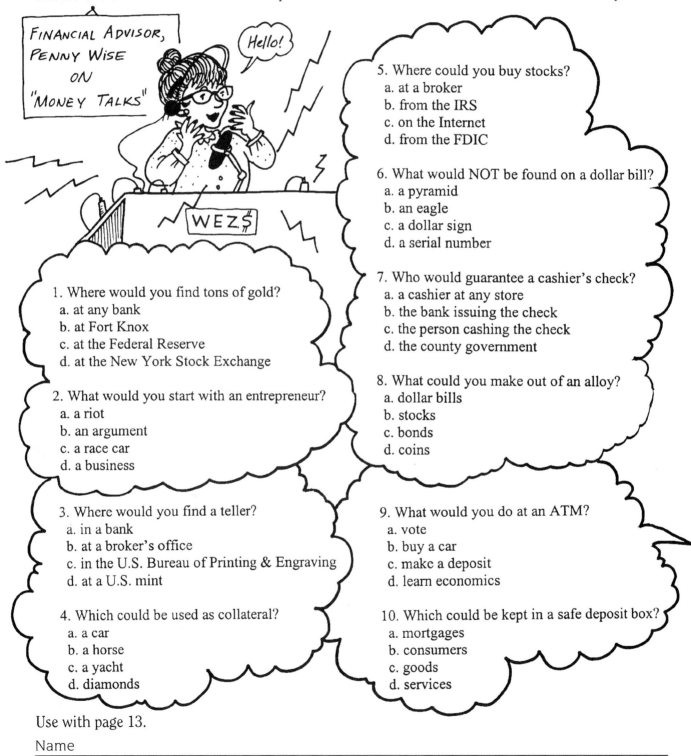

FINANCIAL ADVISOR, PENNY WISE ON "MONEY TALKS"

Hello!

WEZ.$

1. Where would you find tons of gold?
   a. at any bank
   b. at Fort Knox
   c. at the Federal Reserve
   d. at the New York Stock Exchange

2. What would you start with an entrepreneur?
   a. a riot
   b. an argument
   c. a race car
   d. a business

3. Where would you find a teller?
   a. in a bank
   b. at a broker's office
   c. in the U.S. Bureau of Printing & Engraving
   d. at a U.S. mint

4. Which could be used as collateral?
   a. a car
   b. a horse
   c. a yacht
   d. diamonds

5. Where could you buy stocks?
   a. at a broker
   b. from the IRS
   c. on the Internet
   d. from the FDIC

6. What would NOT be found on a dollar bill?
   a. a pyramid
   b. an eagle
   c. a dollar sign
   d. a serial number

7. Who would guarantee a cashier's check?
   a. a cashier at any store
   b. the bank issuing the check
   c. the person cashing the check
   d. the county government

8. What could you make out of an alloy?
   a. dollar bills
   b. stocks
   c. bonds
   d. coins

9. What would you do at an ATM?
   a. vote
   b. buy a car
   c. make a deposit
   d. learn economics

10. Which could be kept in a safe deposit box?
    a. mortgages
    b. consumers
    c. goods
    d. services

Use with page 13.

Name

Choose one or more answers for each question. Choose answers that are reasonable or likely.

11. What would you find at a mint?
    a. coins
    b. certificates of stock
    c. treasury bills
    d. dollar bills

12. Which is LEAST likely to be found at a pawnshop?
    a. a pawnbroker
    b. pastries
    c. jewelry
    d. electronic equipment

13. Which of these can mature?
    a. people
    b. bonds
    c. credit cards
    d. debts

14. Which would NOT be considered a natural resource?
    a. traveler's checks
    b. rushing rivers
    c. old growth forests
    d. city skyscrapers

15. Who is (or was) able to spend continentals?
    a. Presidents Bush, Carter, Clinton, & Reagan
    b. U.S. citizens, during the Civil War
    c. U.S. citizens, from 1775-1783
    d. U.S. citizens, during World War II

16. Whom would you consult for financial advice?
    a. an economist
    b. an agronomist
    c. an astronomer
    d. a biographer

17. Who insures deposits at commercial banks?
    a. the FBI
    b. the CIA
    c. the Federal Trade Commission
    d. the FDIC

18. Which is NOT a transaction?
    a. a deposit at a bank
    b. a withdrawal at a bank
    c. a donation to a blood bank
    d. a loan payment at a bank

19. Which would you prefer to get with the purchase of a new CD player?
    a. a debt
    b. a surcharge
    c. counterfeit change
    d. a warranty

20. Whose face is NOT be found on a U.S. bill?
    a. Andrew Jackson
    b. Abraham Lincoln
    c. George Washington
    d. Susan B. Anthony

21. Who can tell banks to slow down money-lending?
    a. the Social Security Administration
    b. the FDIC
    c. Dow Jones
    d. the Federal Reserve

22. Which would be the LEAST risky?
    a. cosigning a loan for a friend
    b. investing in a new business
    c. buying stocks
    d. putting money into a bank savings account

Hello, Miss Penny Wise? Should I invest in an IRA, a 401K, or just sock it away in my mattress?

Use with page 12.

Name _____

MAKING CHANGE

What do you know about the coins you use? Use your common sense about cents to answer these questions. Write the missing words.

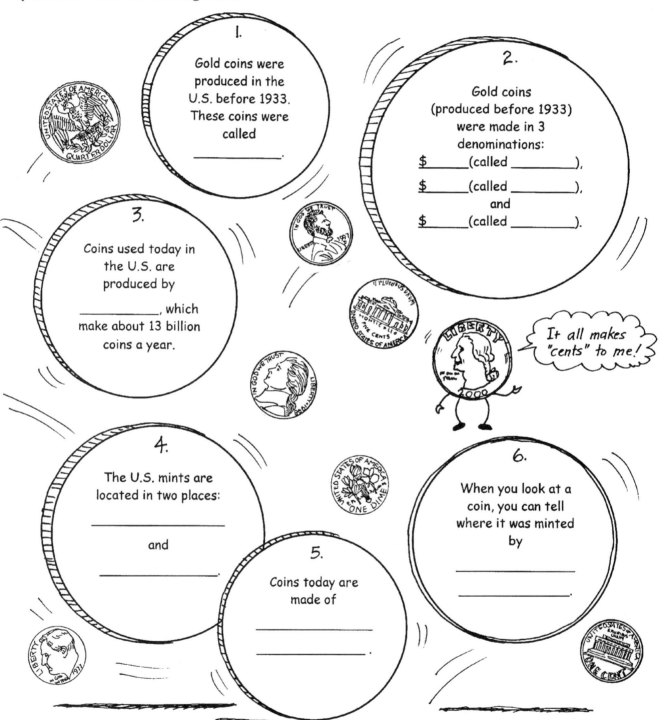

1.
Gold coins were produced in the U.S. before 1933. These coins were called _____.

2.
Gold coins (produced before 1933) were made in 3 denominations:
$_____ (called _____),
$_____ (called _____),
and
$_____ (called _____).

3.
Coins used today in the U.S. are produced by _____, which make about 13 billion coins a year.

4.
The U.S. mints are located in two places:
_____
and
_____

5.
Coins today are made of
_____
_____

6.
When you look at a coin, you can tell where it was minted by
_____
_____.

It all makes "cents" to me!

(Note: Visit the U.S. Mint's website for kids, www2.usmint.gov/Kids, for great information about coins.)

Use with page 15.

Name

Write the missing words.

8.
After some coins are made,
_____
are added to the edges of some, making the coins *milled coins.*

7.
During coin-making, metal is poured into molds to make bars called _____.
These are rolled into flat sheets, and the coins are punched from the sheets.

9.
U.S. milled coins are the
_____
and the
_____.

10.
If you see an **S** or an **O** on a coin, this means that is was minted in one of two cities where there used to be mints. These cities are
_____
and
_____.

13.
The Latin saying on U.S. coins means
_____
_____

11.
Every coin in the U.S. has two sayings stamped on them. The English saying is
_____

12.
Every coin in the U.S. has two sayings stamped on them. The Latin saying is
_____

Use with page 14.

Name _____

DOLLAR SENSE

Banker Bigg dePosit is getting ready to teach a class at a local high school. His topic today is Paper Money in the USA. He is researching these questions to brush up on his facts. Help him get these facts straight.

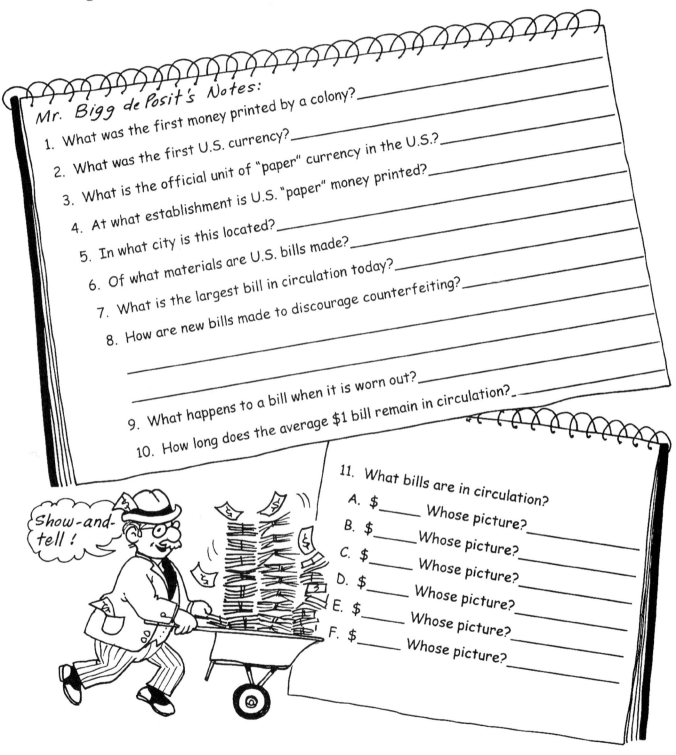

Mr. Bigg dePosit's Notes:

1. What was the first money printed by a colony?_____
2. What was the first U.S. currency?_____
3. What is the official unit of "paper" currency in the U.S.?_____
4. At what establishment is U.S. "paper" money printed?_____
5. In what city is this located?_____
6. Of what materials are U.S. bills made?_____
7. What is the largest bill in circulation today?_____
8. How are new bills made to discourage counterfeiting?_____
_____
_____
9. What happens to a bill when it is worn out?_____
10. How long does the average $1 bill remain in circulation?_____

11. What bills are in circulation?
   A. $_____ Whose picture?_____
   B. $_____ Whose picture?_____
   C. $_____ Whose picture?_____
   D. $_____ Whose picture?_____
   E. $_____ Whose picture?_____
   F. $_____ Whose picture?_____

Show-and-tell!

Use with page 17.

Name

Find a real dollar bill. Examine it carefully. Find out what all the symbols, pictures, numbers, and signatures mean. Then tell what's what for each of the eight places and spaces marked on this dollar bill.

1. What is this number called? _____

   Why is it on a bill? _____

2. Whose signature is this? _____

3. What is this date all about? _____

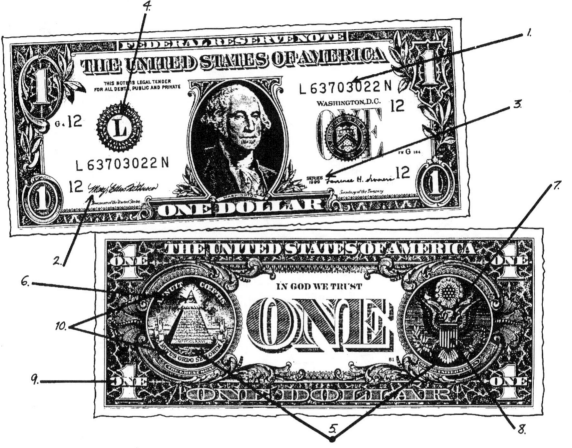

4. What does this mark tell? _____

5. Arrows point to the two sides of what? _____

6. What does the eye symbolize? _____

7. For what does the eagle stand? _____

8. What is the significance of the stripes? _____

9. What does this number mean? _____

10. What is the meaning of the words below?

    A. Annuit coeptis _____

    B. Novus ordo seclorum _____

(Note: Visit the website of the U.S. Bureau of Engraving and Printing,
Use with page 16. *www.bep.treas.gov, for more information about money.)*

Name _____

MONEY-MAKING MIX-UP

Someone turned on the fan in Patricia Proffitt's accounting office. All of the labels blew away from her files on money-making activities. Fix the problem by writing the correct labels back where they belong. Each label is a term that matches a description related to making money.

minimum wage

interest

consumer

wage

training

benefits

bonuses

producers

income

employer

SALARY

investment

employee

Uh, oh!

1. _____ is money a person gets from working, investments or other sources, such as interest.

2. An _____ is a person who works for another person or a company in return for some form of pay.

3. _____ are additional awards, other than pay, given to workers by an employer.

4. An _____ is a company or person who hires others to work for pay.

5. _____ are companies or people who create or provide goods or services in a society.

6. _____ is the lowest amount of money a worker is allowed to be paid under the laws of a state.

7. A _____ is a fixed amount of money paid for work done, usually established at a yearly or monthly rate.

8. _____ is money earned by a person when a bank or someone else pays them for use of their money.

9. _____ is the risk of money or time that someone takes for getting something in return— such as a profit.

10. A _____ is money paid to a worker for work done, often paid at an hourly rate.

Name _____

MONEY-SPENDING MIX-UP

Accountant Patricia Proffitt has again gotten into a mix-up. A fan blew all the labels off her files. These files are all related to spending money. Patricia has glued the labels back on the files, but she may not have gotten them right. Check them out. Cross out any incorrect labels, and write the correct ones in the right places.

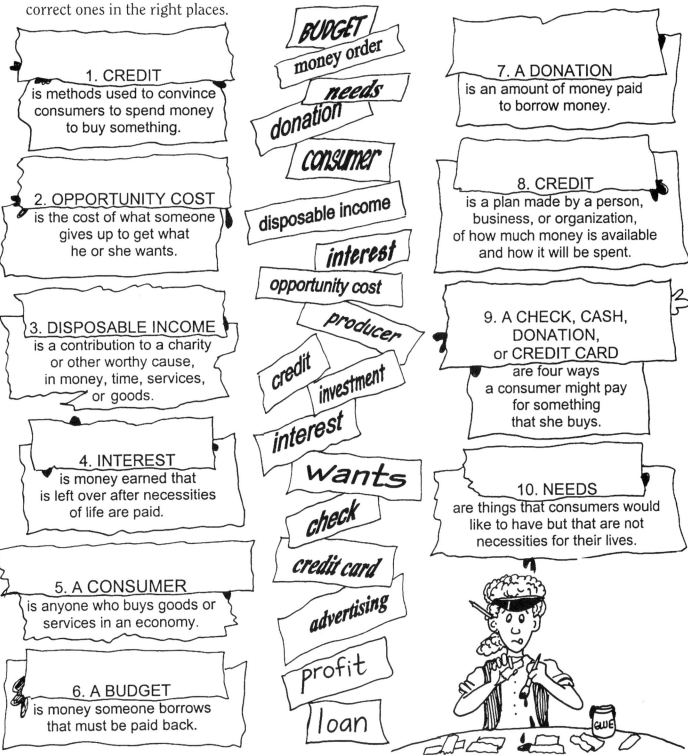

1. CREDIT is methods used to convince consumers to spend money to buy something.

2. OPPORTUNITY COST is the cost of what someone gives up to get what he or she wants.

3. DISPOSABLE INCOME is a contribution to a charity or other worthy cause, in money, time, services, or goods.

4. INTEREST is money earned that is left over after necessities of life are paid.

5. A CONSUMER is anyone who buys goods or services in an economy.

6. A BUDGET is money someone borrows that must be paid back.

7. A DONATION is an amount of money paid to borrow money.

8. CREDIT is a plan made by a person, business, or organization, of how much money is available and how it will be spent.

9. A CHECK, CASH, DONATION, or CREDIT CARD are four ways a consumer might pay for something that she buys.

10. NEEDS are things that consumers would like to have but that are not necessities for their lives.

Labels: BUDGET, money order, needs, donation, consumer, disposable income, interest, opportunity cost, producer, credit, investment, interest, wants, check, credit card, advertising, profit, loan

Name _____

THE JOB MARKET

Job-seekers come by this bulletin board to examine the available jobs. How good are the offers? Use the job notices below to answer the questions on the next page (page 21).

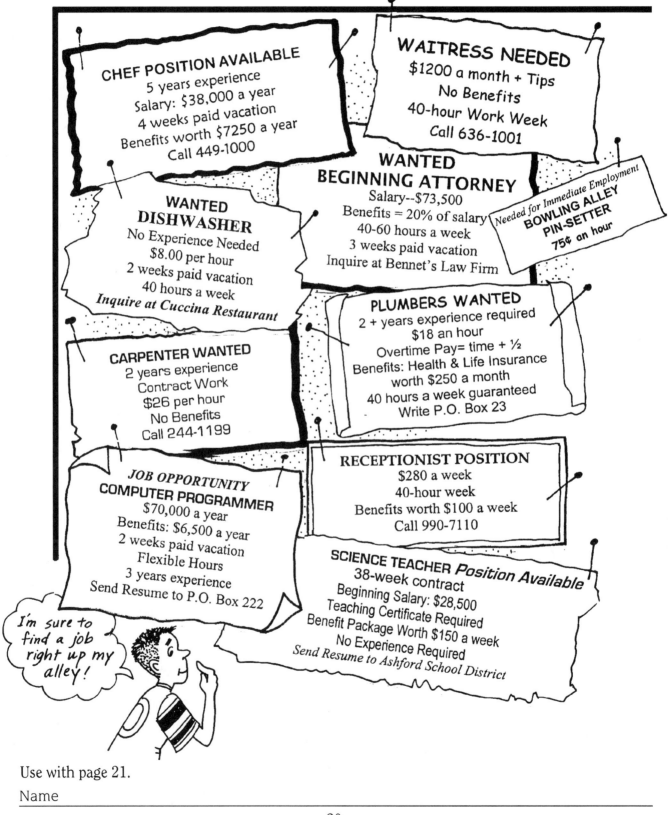

CHEF POSITION AVAILABLE
5 years experience
Salary: $38,000 a year
4 weeks paid vacation
Benefits worth $7250 a year
Call 449-1000

WAITRESS NEEDED
$1200 a month + Tips
No Benefits
40-hour Work Week
Call 636-1001

**WANTED
BEGINNING ATTORNEY**
Salary--$73,500
Benefits = 20% of salary
40-60 hours a week
3 weeks paid vacation
Inquire at Bennet's Law Firm

Needed for Immediate Employment
**BOWLING ALLEY
PIN-SETTER**
75¢ an hour

**WANTED
DISHWASHER**
No Experience Needed
$8.00 per hour
2 weeks paid vacation
40 hours a week
Inquire at Cuccina Restaurant

PLUMBERS WANTED
2 + years experience required
$18 an hour
Overtime Pay= time + ½
Benefits: Health & Life Insurance
worth $250 a month
40 hours a week guaranteed
Write P.O. Box 23

CARPENTER WANTED
2 years experience
Contract Work
$26 per hour
No Benefits
Call 244-1199

RECEPTIONIST POSITION
$280 a week
40-hour week
Benefits worth $100 a week
Call 990-7110

**JOB OPPORTUNITY
COMPUTER PROGRAMMER**
$70,000 a year
Benefits: $6,500 a year
2 weeks paid vacation
Flexible Hours
3 years experience
Send Resume to P.O. Box 222

SCIENCE TEACHER *Position Available*
38-week contract
Beginning Salary: $28,500
Teaching Certificate Required
Benefit Package Worth $150 a week
No Experience Required
Send Resume to Ashford School District

I'm sure to find a job right up my alley!

Use with page 21.

Name

Read the job notices on page 20. Use that information to answer the questions below.

1. Gina decided to take the waitress job advertised. Her first month (4 weeks), she worked 8 hours a day, 5 days a week. She earned an average of $38 a day in tips. How much did she earn in that month?

_____

2. Who will earn more for a 40-hour week of work? *(Include the value of the benefits in your calculations.)*

   a. the receptionist   b. the dishwasher?

3. If Angie takes the teaching job and works 50 hours a week, how much will she earn per hour? *(Include the value of the benefits in your calculations.)*

_____

4. Who will earn more in a year? *(Include the value of the benefits in your calculations.)*
   a. the attorney
   b. the computer programmer?

5. Sam took the carpenter job. He worked 1500 hours in the year. He paid $5600 in taxes and $4100 for health insurance. How much income was left over?

_____

6. Louise took the attorney position. If she works an average of 30 hours a week for the year (49 weeks), what hourly rate will she earn? *(Include the value of the benefits in your calculations.)*

_____

7. Louis took the plumber job. He worked 210 hours the first month. How much did he earn? *(Include the value of the benefits in your calculations.)*

_____

8. What is the approximate weekly rate of income for the chef, calculated over 52 weeks? *(Include the value of the benefits in your calculations.)*

_____

9. If the plumber and the carpenter each work 40 hours a week for 4 weeks, who will earn more: the plumber or the carpenter? *(Include the value of the benefits in your calculations.)*

_____

Astrophysicist?... Brain surgeon?... Eco-biologist?..... Or, pin-setter in a bowling alley?

Hmmm... Hard to choose...

Use with page 20.

Name _____

YOU CAN BANK ON IT!

Cal Q. Layter is puzzled by the banking business. He is always getting the different accounts and numbers confused. This puzzle can straighten out some of his confusion—if he can get the right clues matched to the puzzle solution. He's got the answers in the right places. Help him get the clues labeled correctly.

On the next page, write the location of the word from the puzzle that matches the description.

Use with page 23.

Name

Each word on the puzzle from page 22 matches one of the clues given below. Write the LOCATION of the word next to each clue. (For instance, write 4-A [for ACROSS] or 15-D [for DOWN.])

_____ A. any business done at a bank

_____ B. a check returned for lack of funds

_____ C. an individual retirement account

_____ D. money loaned that must be paid back

_____ E. to take money out of a bank account

_____ F. to put money in a bank account

_____ G. to get bills and coins for a check

_____ H. a kind of check guaranteed by a bank

_____ I. a machine that performs banking operations

_____ J. to sign your name on the back of a check

_____ K. a "space" in a bank where you can keep money

_____ L. papers given to show the amount of deposits

_____ M. money borrowed for a certain amount of time

_____ N. to move money from one place to another

_____ O. a written summary of activities on a bank account

_____ P. the amount of money left in an account at a given time

_____ Q. a code that allows a person to use an ATM card

_____ R. government agency that insures accounts in many banks

_____ S. person who handles money at a bank window

_____ T. money made by a business (after expenses are paid)

_____ U. to move money from a check electronically into an account

_____ V. abbreviation for moving money electronically by computer

_____ W. _____(–deposit box) a locked box to keep special items at a bank

_____ X. the part of a checkbook where deposits and withdrawals are written

_____ Y. smallest amount that must be kept in a bank account to avoid bank fees

_____ Z. special kinds of checks that are used instead of cash by travelers

_____ AA. money paid to borrow money or paid by a bank to depositors for using their money

_____ BB. a written order telling that an amount of money is to be paid to a certain person or business

_____ CC. a certificate for a savings deposit that is left in the bank for a specific amount of time

_____ DD. a sum of money in an account or owed on a loan, not including interest

_____ EE. _____ payments are regular payments made over a specified period of time

_____ FF. a bank card that allows a person to withdraw money from an account electronically

_____ GG. a check endorsement signed by someone other than the person named by the endorsement

_____ HH. a written order to pay money from someone's account to a person or business named on the order

Use with page 22.

Name _____

A BALANCING ACT

I save string, tinfoil, and aluminum. I shop at thrift stores and even cut my own hair. Is it any wonder that I have 10 savings accounts?

Ms. Penny Pincher is terribly proud of her ability to save. She has ten savings accounts. In 2001, she opened a new one at the First National Bank. She is very particular about keeping track of her savings.

Take a peek inside her savings account passbook. Use it to answer the questions below. (Some transactions are missing from her passbook! You'll have to figure out what they are.)

SAVINGS PASSBOOK

Account Number 008-2551

First National Bank

DATE	DEPOSIT	WITHDRAWAL	INTEREST	BALANCE
				$200.00
1-01-01	$200.00		$ 2.50	$202.50
3-30-01				$1202.50
4-01-01	$1000.00		$ 15.03	$1217.53
6-30-01				$583.03
7-05-01				$2003.03
8-18-01				
9-22-01	$345.00		$24.10	
9-30-01				
10-01-01		$110.00		
12-31-01			$32.03	

1. Notice the first interest deposit at the end of the first quarter. What annual interest rate does Ms. Pincher earn?

   _____

2. What transaction took place on July 5?

   _____

3. What transaction took place on August 18?

   _____

4. What was her balance at the end of the day on September 22?

   _____

5. What was her balance at the end of the day on October 1?

   _____

6. What was her balance at the end of the year?

   _____

7. If Penny had made no deposits or withdrawals after January 1, what would her balance have been at the end of the year? (Interest compounded quarterly.)

   a. $10.00   c. $219.00

   b. $210.19   d. $268.00

Use with page 25.

Name

Penny Pincher thinks she knows about all kinds of savings plans. She has accurate figures for all of these questions. See if yours are accurate.

As you can see, my thrifty ways have really payed off for me!

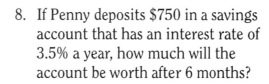

8. If Penny deposits $750 in a savings account that has an interest rate of 3.5% a year, how much will the account be worth after 6 months?

Answer _____

9. Penny buys a $2500 CD which gives an annual interest rate of 7.5 %. Her friend Cassius Bonus puts his $3200 in an account, which gives 5.5% a year. At the end of 18 months, they both withdraw their money and the interest they have earned. Who will withdraw more?

Answer _____

10. Penny opened an account with $50. She saved $50 a month every month for 2 years. At the end of that time, would she have saved enough money to buy a mountain bike that cost $1239.00?

Answer _____

11. If Penny dips into a savings account that has $1375 and takes $15 a week, approximately how many weeks will the account last before it empties out?

Answer _____

12. Penny pays $1200 for a savings bond that gives 9% interest. She keeps the bond for 10 years. About how much will it be worth at the end of 5 years? (Calculate the interest compounded at the end of each year.)

Answer _____

13. Cassius pays $7500 for a bond that gives 6% interest. He cashes the bond in after 3 years. Penny buys a bond for $5000. It yields 5% interest. She keeps it for 5 years. Which bond will be worth the most when it is cashed?

Answer _____

14. Penny opened a shopping savings account on January 1 with a deposit of $100. After that, she deposited an amount of money on the 15th of each month (including January). On December 1, she withdrew all the money--$925.00. How much did she save each month? (Do not include interest.)

Answer _____

Use with page 24.

Name _____

CHECKS & BALANCES

Moe Monnie is always spending money.
He always wishes he had more. Maybe it's because he spends too much!
He does try to keep his checkbook balanced, however. Most of the time he does a good job of it.
This is his check register. Use it to answer the questions.

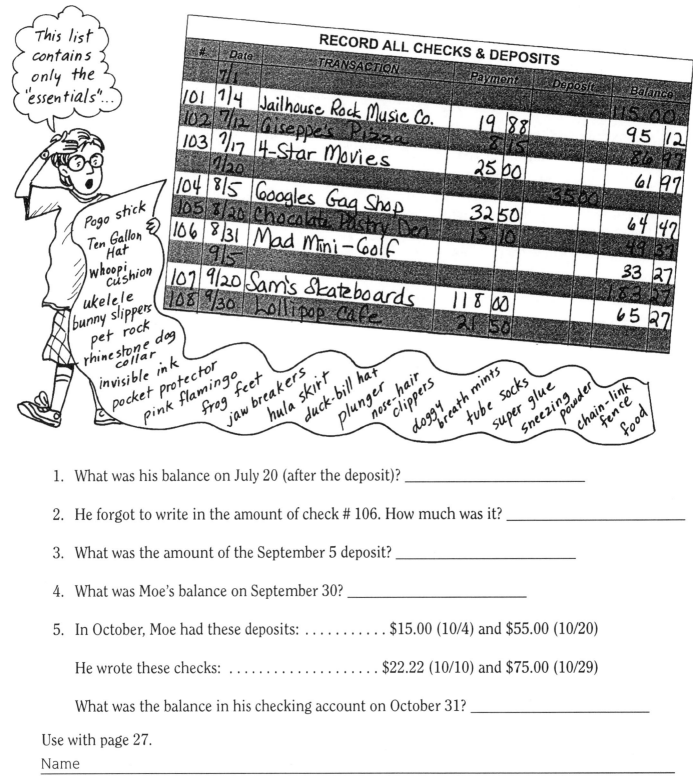

This list contains only the "essentials"...

Pogo stick
Ten Gallon Hat
whoopi cushion
ukelele
bunny slippers
pet rock
rhinestone dog collar
invisible ink
pocket protector
pink flamingo
frog feet
jaw breakers
hula skirt
duck-bill hat
plunger
nose-hair clippers
doggy breath mints
tube socks
super glue
sneezing powder
chain-link fence
food

#	Date	RECORD ALL CHECKS & DEPOSITS TRANSACTION	Payment		Deposit		Balance	
	7/1							
101	7/4	Jailhouse Rock Music Co.					115	00
102	7/12	Giseppe's Pizza	19	88			95	12
103	7/17	4-Star Movies	8	15			86	97
	7/20		25	00			61	97
104	8/5	Googles Gag Shop			35	00		
105	8/20	Chocolate Pastry Den	32	50			64	47
106	8/31	Mad Mini-Golf	15	10			49	37
	9/5						33	27
107	9/20	Sam's Skateboards	118	00			183	27
108	9/30	Lollipop Cafe	21	50			65	27

1. What was his balance on July 20 (after the deposit)? _____

2. He forgot to write in the amount of check # 106. How much was it? _____

3. What was the amount of the September 5 deposit? _____

4. What was Moe's balance on September 30? _____

5. In October, Moe had these deposits: . . . . $15.00 (10/4) and $55.00 (10/20)

    He wrote these checks: . . . . $22.22 (10/10) and $75.00 (10/29)

    What was the balance in his checking account on October 31? _____

Use with page 27.

Name _____

Track down the information you will need about checking accounts to settle these questions about Moe's banking activities.

6. When Moe opened his checking account, he needed to learn how to write a check. Which of these things would he probably NOT write on his check?
    a. the date   b. his birthday   c. his signature

7. Moe wrote a check to pay a parking ticket, which of these things would he probably NOT write on the check?
    a. the amount of money being paid
    b. the number of the parking ticket
    c. an excuse for why he let the parking meter run out

8. On his check, how many times will Moe need to write the amount of money that the check pays? _____

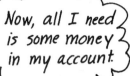

Now, all I need is some money in my account.

Moe has learned about the many numbers on his check.
Get someone to share a check with you so you can examine it.

9. Moe always finds a number in the upper right hand corner. This is different on each check.

This number tells_____.

10. There are numbers along the bottom of Moe's checks. Tell what these numbers are for:

_____

11. In November, Moe had a birthday. Aunt Lotta Monnie gave him a check for his birthday. When Moe deposited

it into his account, he endorsed the check. Tell what this means:_____

12. In December, Moe got carried away at the snowboard shop. He bought some equipment that was out

of his budget range. He wrote a check for $125.00. He overdrew his checking account.

Explain what that means:_____

13. When Moe overdrew his account, his check bounced. Explain what that means:_____

_____

14. A traveler's check is a special kind of check. Tell how traveler's checks work:_____

_____

15. A cashier's check is another special kind of check. Explain what a cashier's check is:_____

_____

Use with page 26.

Name

THE CREDIT GAME

Patricia Profitt has been busy using credit to get a lot of the goods she wants. It could be a risky game she's playing with all these loans! You can find out about what she's been doing by playing this credit game (on this page and page 29). Play it alone or with a friend.

Get two coins. Toss one coin to land on the board below. Read the credit situation. Find the square on the next board (page 29) that describes what Patricia has done. Place the second coin on that square.

I'm cutting off this line of credit!

1. The bank has agreed to loan Patricia money, but they're holding the title to her boat until her loan is paid off.	2. Borrowing money has a price. Pat bought a new sound system on credit, and she must pay 8% interest.	3. A bank has given Patricia a card that allows her to buy things now and pay later.	4. Patricia bought a new computer. The store financed it for her. The smallest payment she can make each month is $50.
5. A bank has agreed that Patricia can borrow up to $2000 any time she needs money.	6. Patricia just went to a bank and borrowed money by giving only a credit history and her signature.	7. Patricia bought a new motorbike. She made a down payment of $100, and must pay $30 a month at 9% interest.	8. Patricia has charged as much on her credit card as the credit card company will allow her.
9. Patricia has failed to pay a loan according to her agreement.	10. Patricia is shocked to learn that the finance charge on her credit card is 21 ½ % a year.	11. Patricia has just signed an agreement to borrow money from a bank to buy a piece of property.	12. Patricia has bought a $2000 car that she paid for with someone else's money. She owes the money for this car to her friend.
13. A credit card company allows Patricia to get cash from her card. She can get cash at a machine, or write herself a check.	14. On the 15th of every month, Patricia must pay $35 on the debt owed for her new snowboard.	15. She had spent so much money that her credit was weak, so Pat needed someone else to sign along with her for her latest loan.	16. Patricia paid a lump sum of money as the first payment when she signed the loan agreement for her new skis.

Use with page 29.

Name _____

Use two coins. Toss one coin to land on the board on page 28. Read the credit situation. Find the square on this board that describes what Patricia has done. Place the second coin on that square.

Right this way, ladies and gentlemen. Everything's on sale. Buy now—pay later!

Sam Slick-Salesman

CREDIT DEPT. →

A. She has signed for an unsecured loan.	B. She has made a down payment on a loan.	C. She has reached her credit limit.	D. Patricia has defaulted on a debt.
E. Something valuable she owns is being used as collateral for a loan.	F. Patricia has just gotten a credit card.	G. She must make installment payments on a purchase.	H. Patricia has arranged for a mortgage.
I. Patricia has agreed to a series of credit terms.	J. She has just been given a line of credit.	K. Patricia needed someone to cosign for a loan.	L. Patricia has a debt of $2000.
M. The loan agreement has set a minimum payment for each month.	N. One of the terms of her credit purchase is an 8% finance charge.	O. The annual interest percentage rate on this credit card is a high one.	P. Patricia has a credit card that offers cash advances.

Use with page 28.

Name

QUESTIONS OF INTEREST

Lottie O'Dollars seems to be surrounded by interest payments. She pays interest on loans, credit cards, and purchases. She gets interest on bank accounts and loans to her friends. She's loaded with interest computations and questions.

Here are some possible answers to her interest questions. But what are the questions?
Read the "questions of interest" on the next page (page 31).
Find the answer here that belongs with each question. Write the letter of the correct answer by its matching question.

1. Lottie's friend, Lester Spender, has borrowed $50 from her at 10% interest. She calculates the interest at the end of each year, and adds the interest to the amount owed. If Lester makes no payments until three years have ended, how much will he owe Lottie at the end of the three years?

_____

2. At the beginning of the new year, Lottie bought a savings bond that cost $100. The 10% interest is calculated at the end of a year's time, and the interest is added to the principal. How many years will it take for her money to double?

_____

3. Last summer, Lottie bought a treadmill for $2000. She financed it with the store at 8% interest a year. The store calculates interest at the end of each year. Yesterday, after exactly one year, Lottie made a payment of $300. This covered all the interest for the year. The rest of the payment went toward paying down the principal of the loan. How much principal is left to pay on the loan?

_____

Use with page 31.

Name _____

Here are some "questions of interest." But where are the answers? You'll find the correct answers mixed in among some misleading answers on the previous page (page 30). Find the answer there that belongs with each question. Write the letter of the correct answer by its matching question.

I'm interested in shopping with my credit card — but the interest is too high!

4. The interest on Lottie's credit card is 24% a year. Interest begins to accumulate the day a purchase is made. She used the card to buy a $190 calculator on April 1. Exactly 30 days later, the credit card company sent her a bill. How much interest had accumulated on her purchase in that month?

_____

5. Lottie found just the car she needed. The price was $13,500. The car dealer wanted to give her a loan for the full amount at 6% for a year. Lottie's Uncle Len loaned her the money at no interest. How much did Lottie save in a year by borrowing from Uncle Len instead of the bank?

_____

6. Lottie is trying to save $2000 to go on a 10-week expedition to search for Bigfoot. She bought a $1300 CD (certificate of deposit) that earned her 4.5% interest. The interest was added to the account at the end of each year. She made no deposits or withdrawals for a year while interest accumulated. At the end of a year, she began to add $15 a week to the account. How long after the end of that year will it take her to reach her goal of $2000?

_____

7. Six months after Lottie borrowed some money from a bank, the interest due was $24.00. She borrowed the money at 12% interest, which was calculated every 6 months. What was the amount of the loan?

_____

Use with page 30.

Name

BUDGET BLUES

Wanna Splurge has the budget blues. Actually, she has no budget! Without one, her finances are like a money-sucking machine. It seems there is never quite enough money coming in to meet all her needs and wants!

Review the details of her finances. Help Wanna make choices by planning a one-month budget that will work for her. Use the notebook on the next page (page 33) to make the plan for July.

MONEY IN

JULY INCOME SOURCES

Job Income	$ 1916
Graduation Gifts	$ 300
Prize Money	$ 75
Tax Rebate	$ 250

Necessities:

Rent	$ 550
Car Payment	$ 175
Utilities	$ 210
Car Insurance	$ 80
Gas & Car Expenses	$ 130
Medical Insurance	$ 110
Food	$ 225
Loan Payments	$ 160
Credit Card Payment	$ 75
Taxes	$ 300
Allergy Medicine	$ 25

Other:

Clothing	$ 150
Recreation	$ 100
Eating Out	$ 75
Savings	$ 50
Trip to Chicago	$ 100
Dog Food	$ 30
Donations	$ 75
New Bike	$ 400
Health Club Dues	$ 45
Gifts for Friends	$ 75

MONEY LEFT

SAVINGS

Use with page 33.

Name

Read about Wanna's incoming and outgoing money for July (on page 32). Make a budget that will work for her for the month of July. Make choices about how Wanna can spend her money this month.

July Budget

MONEY IN:

_____

_____

_____

_____

Total: _____

MONEY OUT:

_____

_____

_____

_____

_____

_____

_____

_____

_____

_____

_____

_____

Total: _____

Notes:
Sell in-line skates for $75.⁰⁰

Penny owes me $125.⁰⁰. She promised to pay me back in July.

If I car-pool to work with Nan, I can cut my gas bill in half.

An emergency trip to the Vet cost me $135.⁰⁰!!

Make two suggestions to Wanna that may help her live within her budget in future months.

1. _____

_____

2. _____

_____

Use with page 32.

Name _____

WHAT'S THE CONSEQUENCE?

For every decision Penny makes about earning, spending, saving, investing, or giving away money, she gives up something and she gets something. These are the consequences (or costs) and benefits of economic decisions.

Write one or more consequences and one or more benefits for each of the economic decisions described here and on page 35.

What a way to stretch a dollar!

1. Penny has saved $500 over the past six months. She has been searching for a leather jacket. At the department store, she can get a new one in the latest style for $398. Or, she can get one of a lesser quality at a discount store, and spend $210. A second-hand store has a well-worn leather jacket that fits Penny. It costs $88. Penny chooses to buy the jacket at the discount store.

What are the benefits of this decision?

_____

_____

What are the consequences (costs)?

_____

_____

2. Lenny O'Coin has been searching for a job. He was offered a job cooking at a fast food restaurant. The schedule is a hard one; the job hours are 7–11 A.M. and 4–8 P.M. five days a week. The pay is $12 an hour, plus insurance for him. The other job offer he received is for pet care. He can set his own schedule and work up to 40 hours a week for $10 an hour. There is no insurance provided. Lenny chooses the pet care job.

What are the benefits of this decision?

_____

_____

What are the consequences (costs)?

_____

_____

3. For her vacation, Josie Driver could fly from Seattle to Nashville for $550. She calculated that this trip would take her 11 hours. She figured it would cost about $350 in gas, food, and motels if she made the trip by car. This trip would take her 3 days. She chose to drive to Nashville.

What are the benefits of this decision?

_____

_____

What are the consequences (costs)?

_____

_____

OUCH!

Use with page 35.

Name _____

34

4. For a year, Harvey Kares spent $25 a month to belong to a health club. Then he heard that a few dollars a month could feed a starving child in a third-world country. Now Harvey gives that $25 each month to a charity that helps save children.

What are the benefits of this decision?

_____

_____

What are the consequences (costs)?

_____

_____

5. J. D. Racer, a high school student, decides to buy a car for $1800. He figures this will save him time because he'll be able to get to school in 15 minutes, instead of riding the school bus 45 minutes each way. However, to have a car, he must get a job after school and on weekends. He will need to work 20 hours a week to pay for his gasoline and car insurance.

What are the benefits of this decision?

_____

_____

What are the consequences (costs)?

_____

_____

America needs a good "cents" fiscal policy!

6. The banker, Mr. de Posit, spent $150 on food each month. He also spent a lot of time cooking-and he hated it! (He was a terrible cook, anyway.) He decided to eat all his dinners out. Now he spends $275 a month on food.

What are the benefits of this decision?

_____

_____

What are the consequences (costs)?

_____

_____

7. Moe Monnie considered buying a motor-bike that would cost him $60 a month for two years with 8% interest. It was the latest really cool-looking model. He also considered a used bike. This would cost $40 a month for one year with no interest. It worked fine and looked okay, but it was not as fast or as great-looking. It also did not have a warranty that comes with a new bike. Moe chose the older bike.

What are the benefits of this decision?

_____

_____

What are the consequences (costs)?

_____

_____

Use with page 34.

Name _____

TOUGH CHOICES

Today's classified ads are exceptionally exciting for Brenda Buyer. She has found all kinds of great stuff she has wanted to get at good prices. Like most of us, Brenda cannot buy everything she wants, so she has to make some choices.

> Brenda has $800 in a savings account, and $180 in cash.
> Read the ads on page 37, and use the information to answer
> the questions about Brenda's choices.
> *(Each question assumes that she has not bought anything else yet.)*

1.
How much will Brenda need to take from her savings if she buys the keyboard?

_____

2.
If Brenda buys a puppy and the CD collection, will she have to take money from savings?

_____

3.
Can she buy the gum ball machine and two pairs of jeans with the cash she has?

_____

4.
Brenda hopes to buy the scuba equipment and a mouse pad. Can she also buy jeans and two pizzas without dipping into her savings?

_____

5.
After looking over the ads, Brenda thinks she might skip the expensive items. Instead, she considers spending on the cheaper things. Can she play miniature golf (taking a friend), see a movie, get two pizzas, order a mouse pad, buy a dozen doughnuts, get a pet cricket, and sign up for karate lessons using the cash she has on hand?

_____

6.
If Brenda buys the lawnmower, how much will be left in her savings account (assuming she also uses all of her cash)?

_____

7.
Brenda wants to leave at least $500 in her savings account. Can she take karate lessons if she buys the video camera and the trampoline?

_____

8. Brenda is thinking about buying the skates, the keyboard, and the video camera. Is it a good idea for her to spend the amount of money these would cost? Tell why or why not.

_____

How far can my money go?

Use with page 37.

Name _____

TRAMPOLINE FOR SALE
11-ft round
trampoline
2 years old
In great shape
$75
Call 662-9777

SCUBA GEAR
Great Deal!!
Only Slightly Used
Men's Size Medium
Wet Suit
Fins
Mask
Tanks
Gages
Gloves
$130
Call C. Gye
663-1243

KARATE LESSONS
$45 for 10 Weeks
Qualified Instructors
We take students
ages 6-60.
Classes:
T, W, TH
6 – 8 am and 4-6 pm
Up-Town
Karate Studio
221 South Amherst
Call 317-0877
for more information

HUSKY PUPPIES
Pure White Puppies
6 weeks old
Paper-Trained
$85
Call 209-5687

Miniature Golf
$14 for two
PUTTER'S PARADISE
1616 Kings Hwy
Hours:
11 am – midnight
7 days a week

PET CRICKETS
Yes!
Crickets make great
pets!
Easy to Keep
Enjoyable Music
Buy Several!
$2.00 each
Call D. Cheerp
662-5242

CD COLLECTION
For Sale
100 CDs
ROCK MUSIC
of the 1990s
In good condition
$150
Call Ted
For list of CDs e-mail
Ted@singsong.net

VIDEO CAMERA
Re-Conditioned
Late Model
Must Sell
Purchased @ $550
Will sell for $200
Call Fran
209-5656

RIDE-ON LAWNMOWER
$416
Like new!
Built-In CD Player
Call 317-3333

DESIGNER JEANS
for sale
All designers
Latest Styles
All Sizes
$27 for any pair
Judy's Jeans
3116 Riverside
Visit our Store
OR
Order Online
www.judyjean.net

MOVIES
$4.00
Tightwad Tuesday
SPECIAL DEAL
All Movies
All Day
Red Corner Theater

BEST PIZZA IN TOWN
Giant Cheese Pizzas
2 for $16
Call 50-PIZZA
We Deliver

ICE SKATES
USED 1 year
Women's Size 6
Worth $500
Sell for $150
Call Gina
552-1000

You Bring the Photo.
We'll make a
MOUSE PAD.
Any Photo
Ready in 1 Day
$18
Jan's Quick Photo
6300 First St.

Milkshake Mixer
Brand New
Never Used
Make
Your
Own
Shakes!
Instructions Included
$60
Call Mike
662-7578

ELECTRONIC KEYBOARD
Used Only 6-months
Top Brand
Was $1800 new
NOW $600
Call Deano for
Demonstration
662-0909

GUM BALL MACHINE
Electronic
Lights flash with
each gum ball
$100
Holds 1000 gum balls
Call Tom: 209-7654

Doughnut Special
MONDAYS
All Day
$2 a dozen
Round N Round Pastry
666 Front St

Use with page 36.

DUBIOUS SPEECHES

A lot of people are in the dark about the way the economy works. These two economists share their ideas very loudly. They often try to out-do each other with their brilliance. Are they in the dark, too?

Read the speeches given by Dr. Bill Bucks and Dr. Theodora Thrift. Decide if each statement is correct. If it is, circle the number. If it is NOT correct, be ready to discuss the errors with any other friends or students of economics around you. (Use this page with page 39).

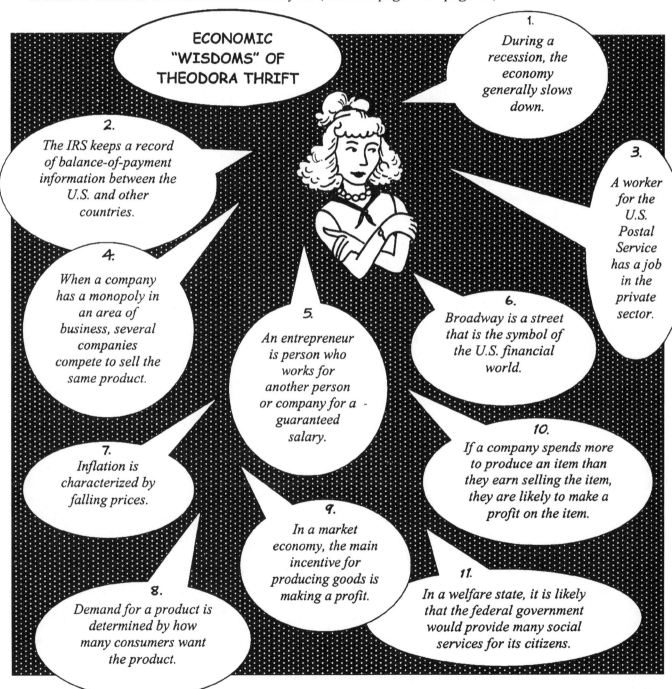

ECONOMIC "WISDOMS" OF THEODORA THRIFT

1. During a recession, the economy generally slows down.

2. The IRS keeps a record of balance-of-payment information between the U.S. and other countries.

3. A worker for the U.S. Postal Service has a job in the private sector.

4. When a company has a monopoly in an area of business, several companies compete to sell the same product.

5. An entrepreneur is person who works for another person or company for a guaranteed salary.

6. Broadway is a street that is the symbol of the U.S. financial world.

7. Inflation is characterized by falling prices.

8. Demand for a product is determined by how many consumers want the product.

9. In a market economy, the main incentive for producing goods is making a profit.

10. If a company spends more to produce an item than they earn selling the item, they are likely to make a profit on the item.

11. In a welfare state, it is likely that the federal government would provide many social services for its citizens.

Use with page 39.

Name

Read the speeches given by Dr. Bill Bucks and Dr. Theodora Thrift. Decide if each statement is correct. If it is, circle the number. If it is NOT correct, be ready to discuss the errors with any other friends or students of economics around you. (Use this page with page 38).

Use with page 38.

Name

WHAT WILL HAPPEN NEXT?

The workings of the U.S. economy are extremely complex. Some basic principles and concepts help the average citizen understand a bit of it, though. It helps to know something about the way a market economy functions. Brush up on what you know about the laws of supply and demand, the roles of competition and specialization, and how these things affect prices and workers. Put your economic intelligence to work to tackle these economic dilemmas.

This economics student, Elmer Price, has just finished a test on some questions about the workings of the economy. How did he do? Circle the number of each item that he answered correctly. If his answer is wrong, circle the correct answer (or answers).

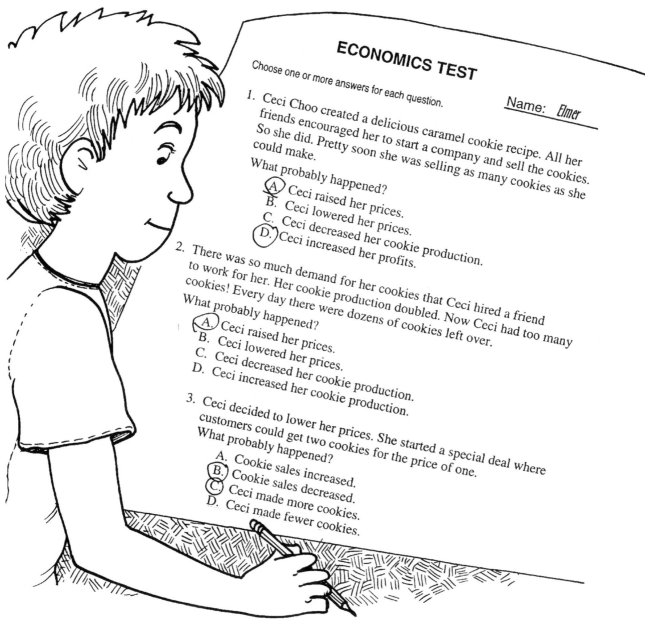

ECONOMICS TEST

Choose one or more answers for each question.

Name: _Elmer_

1. Ceci Choo created a delicious caramel cookie recipe. All her friends encouraged her to start a company and sell the cookies. So she did. Pretty soon she was selling as many cookies as she could make.
   What probably happened?
   A. Ceci raised her prices.
   B. Ceci lowered her prices.
   C. Ceci decreased her cookie production.
   D. Ceci increased her profits.

2. There was so much demand for her cookies that Ceci hired a friend to work for her. Her cookie production doubled. Now Ceci had too many cookies! Every day there were dozens of cookies left over.
   What probably happened?
   A. Ceci raised her prices.
   B. Ceci lowered her prices.
   C. Ceci decreased her cookie production.
   D. Ceci increased her cookie production.

3. Ceci decided to lower her prices. She started a special deal where customers could get two cookies for the price of one.
   What probably happened?
   A. Cookie sales increased.
   B. Cookie sales decreased.
   C. Ceci made more cookies.
   D. Ceci made fewer cookies.

Use with page 41.

Name

Finish examining Elmer's test. Circle the number of correct answers. If his answer for an item is wrong, circle the correct answer (or answers).

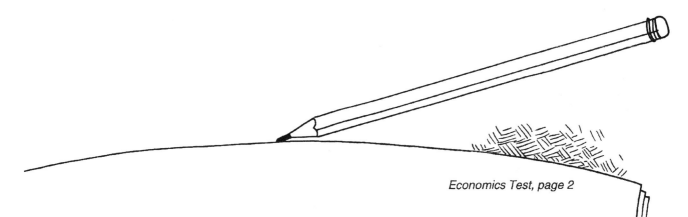

Economics Test, page 2

4. Ceci's cookie business continued to grow and make good profits. Soon some other entrepreneurs in town decided to get in on the profits. Three other cookie companies started business.

   What probably happened?

   A. There was greater choice for customers.
   B. Cookie prices increased.
   C. Cookie prices decreased.
   D. Ceci increased production of cookies.

5. A health & fitness club moved into town and attracted a lot of members. People started thinking cookies were not so good for them. They stopped buying so many cookies.

   What probably happened?

   A. Cookie prices increased.
   B. The cookie companies made larger amounts of cookies.
   C. Profits decreased for the cookie businesses.
   D. Cookie prices decreased.

6. Ceci decided to add healthy foods to her business. She began selling whole-grain muffins, low-fat scones, and sugarless cookies. She added fruit juices and mineral waters to her menus. Before long, her products were in high demand again, and she ran out of baked goods every day before the end of business hours. Her business increased so much, that all the other cookie companies could not compete any longer. They all went out of business.

   What probably happened next?

   A. Ceci's prices increased.
   B. Ceci's prices decreased
   C. Ceci's profits increased.
   D. Customers stopped buying Ceci's products.

Use with page 40.

Name

INCENTIVES WITH POWER

Moe Money can't escape his economy! Everywhere he turns, there are powerful incentives to spend, save, invest, or give away his money. Every decision he makes about money is connected to some incentive, either positive or negative.

Think about these decisions Moe must make. Figure out what the incentives might be for different economic behaviors for Moe.

> Moe has been given a birthday gift of $500. He is usually out of money, so he imagines how nice it would be to have $500 in the bank. This month, the bank's interest rate is up; he can get a certificate of deposit that guarantees him 5%. Then a friend comes along with a cool new skateboard. He learns that these are on sale for $450 this week. Moe's skateboard looks shabby next to his friend's new model.

1. What are the positive incentives for Moe to save the money?

   _____

   _____

2. What are the negative incentives for this same action (incentives NOT to save)?

   _____

   _____

3. What are the positive incentives for Moe to buy the skateboard?

   _____

   _____

4. What are the negative incentives for this same action?

   _____

   _____

> Moe's car is in bad shape. It runs (some of the time). It gets him where he needs to go (most of the time). But it is unreliable. Frequently, he needs help getting it started, or he needs to spend money to get something fixed. Also, Moe is rather embarrassed about the way his car looks. All his friends have better cars. He would like a newer car. To get one, he would have to borrow money from a bank, pay interest, and have a monthly payment of about $150.

5. What are the positive incentives for Moe to keep his old car?

   _____

   _____

6. What are the negative incentives for Moe to keep his old car?

   _____

   _____

Use with page 43.

Name _____

42

Wow! These specs are hot!

Moe's good friend, Lenny O'Coin, is starting a new business selling sunglasses. These glasses have wild, colorful designs. Lenny wants Moe to be a partner by investing $300 to buy the glasses. He gives Moe convincing speeches about how much money they will make on this business. Moe knows these glasses are the hot fashion right now. He also knows that fashions change, and that his friend Lenny is always cooking up some new money scheme.

7. What are the positive incentives for Moe to invest?

_____

8. What are the negative incentives for the same action?

_____

_____

The stock market has always interested Moe. He has noticed that a computer software company, *Hot Games*, has stock that is climbing in value. He is thinking about taking all of his money out of his bank savings account and using it to buy this stock.

9. What are the positive incentives for Moe to buy the stock?

_____

10. What are the negative incentives for the same action?

_____

_____

Several of Moe's neighbors are trying to raise money to help a neighbor child who needs an expensive medical treatment for his cancer. Moe has $75 that he was planning to use to buy tickets to see his favorite musical group in concert. All of his friends are going to the concert. They are planning a fun weekend taking this trip to the concert together.

11. What are the positive incentives for Moe to donate to the cancer treatment fund?

_____

12. What are the negative incentives for the same action?

_____

_____

Use with page 42.

Name _____

TAXING ISSUES

So many taxes! Brenda Buyer has been pondering over her budget. She pays taxes to her city, her state, and her federal government. She realizes that she pays more in taxes than she spends to eat! Join her in pondering some issues about taxes.

WAYS WE USE TAX MONEY

roads
national defense
state parks
government
employees

1. Brenda is making a list of the ways her tax money is used. Add at least five more things to Brenda's list.

_____

_____

_____

_____

_____

2. In Brenda's state, there is a 8.5% sales tax on all items except food and medicine. This week she bought $85 worth of food, a blender for $29, a dog kennel for $65, and a new car for $7150. How much sales tax did she pay?

Answer: _____

3. In her city, there is a 2% tax on business equipment. For her business, Brenda has two computers, each worth $1000, a fax machine worth $350, and two printers, each worth $600. How much tax will Brenda pay this year on her equipment?

Answer: _____

4. Brenda's city also adds a 9% tourist tax to charges at hotels and motels. When Brenda's sister came to visit, she stayed in a hotel for 4 nights. The room cost $89 a night before taxes. Add the sales tax (8.5% of room charge) and the room tax (9% of room charge) to her sister's costs. How much was the total bill for the hotel stay?

Answer: _____

5. Brenda earns $ 18,000 a year, paid to her in 12 monthly payments. Last year, she was taxed 15% in income tax by the federal government and 6% by the state government. How much of her income was left after taxes?

Answer: _____

Use with page 45.

Name _____

Since so much of her income goes to pay taxes, Brenda is learning about different kinds of taxes, and how they work. Help her out by matching the tax-related word with its description. Write the correct letter for each description below.

_____ 6. Money paid in taxes by incorporated businesses

_____ 7. An extra cost added on to the original cost of an item

_____ 8. Money received from employment

_____ 9. Excused from having to pay taxes

_____ 10. The report people file when they pay income taxes

_____ 11. A tax that people pay on the money they make throughout the year

_____ 12. Money received from gifts or investments such as stocks, bonds, or savings accounts

_____ 13. A tax on the sale of goods and some services, usually added to the price of the item

_____ 14. A tax-supported federal system of financial support for retired workers

_____ 15. Companies pay taxes on the amount of this that they make.

_____ 16. A tax-supported federal or state system of financial support for those unable to earn a minimum amount for living

A. WELFARE

B. SOCIAL SECURITY

C. PROFIT

D. CORPORATE TAXES

E. EARNED INCOME

F. NON-PROFIT

G. SURCHARGE

H. SALES TAX

I. TAX-EXEMPT

J. TAX RETURN

K. INCOME TAX

L. UNEARNED INCOME

M. MEDICARE

_____ 17. A group that is not formed for the purpose of making profit (*Examples: a church or charitable organization*)

_____ 18. A tax-supported federal system of financial support for medical insurance and care

Use with page 44.

Name _____

THE MONEY-WATCHERS

Economist Theodora Thrift is, again, making confident statements about money matters in the nation and world. Here she is making notes for a lecture on U.S. money matters, including her wisdom about the Fed. Some things are missing from her statements. Finish each one correctly.

1. The complete name of the Fed is _____.

2. The program followed in influencing money flow is called the Fed's _____ policy.

3. The committee that administers the F.R.S is called_____.
   Its members are appointed by _____ for terms of _____years.

4. The committee that makes the main decisions on policies is the _____.

5. The Fed gets its funding from_____.

6. The Fed reports to _____ but is free to make its own decisions.

7. The Fed has _____ banks, each operating in one of the country's Federal Reserve districts.

8. The Fed works to promote economic growth and control inflation. It does this by influencing the availability of money through controlling _____rates.

9. In periods of rapid economic expansion, the Fed would probably _____interest rates.

10. In periods of recession, the Fed would probably _____interest rates.

11. The Fed is likely to raise the reserve requirement for its banks during periods of economic_____.

12. If the Fed lowers the reserve requirements for its banks, the result will be

    a) _____(more, less) money in circulation.

    b) _____(lower, higher) interest rates for loans.

    c) _____(lower, higher) interest rates on savings accounts.

    d) money that is _____(easier, harder) to borrow.

Use with page 47.

Name _____

This time, Theodora is making notes for her lecture about global economics. She has written each statement with great confidence. Does she have all her facts right? Circle the numbers of the statements that are accurate. Be ready to explain what is wrong about the ones you do not circle.

13. A nation's balance of trade is the amount of goods it exports to other countries.

14. A nation's GNP measures all production of goods and services by firms owned by the nation's citizens during a given period, even if the firms are not located within the country.

15. The International Monetary Fund is an organization that insures bank account deposits by foreigners in U.S. banks.

16. A nation's GDP measures all the goods and services produced within a country in a given period, even those produced by companies that are not owned by citizens of the nation.

17. A nation's balance of payments is the difference between the amount it spends in foreign currencies and the amount of foreign money it takes in.

18. An exchange rate is the price of one country's foreign currency expressed in terms of another country's currency.

19. The United Nations is not a relief organization; it provides no monetary assistance to any country.

20. If a nation has a large balance-of-payments surplus, that nation's currency is likely to decline in its foreign exchange rate.

21. The FTC is an international organization that regulates trade among nations.

22. If a nation has a balance-of-payments deficit, its currency is likely to decline in its foreign exchange rate.

23. Maria, a U.S. citizen, wishes to buy a car in Japan. The cost is 1,350,000 yen. If the exchange rate is 90 yen to one U.S. dollar, she will need $12,000 U.S. dollars to change into yen in order to buy the car.

24. In a nation that has a developing economy, you would expect to find all of these factors:
    - a lower GNP
    - a lower rate of literacy
    - high population growth
    - high life expectancy
    - limited industrialization

Use with page 46.

Name _____

WORLD-WIDE MONEY MATTERS

Although economies all over the world differ in many ways, they share many features.
The table shows the details of some of the common features that make up the financial matters of most nations. Use the information to answer the questions on page 49.

FINANCIAL DATA from SELECTED NATIONS

Country	GDP	GDP per capita	Inflation Rate	Unemploy-ment Rate	Exports	Imports	Economic Aid
Angola	$11.6 billion	$1.030	270%	substantial	$5 billion	$3 billion	Recipient $493.1 million
Australia	$416.2 billion	$22.200	1.8%	7.5%	$58 billion	$67 billion	Donor $1.43 billion
Belarus	$55.2 billion	$5,300	295%	2.3%	$6 billion	$6.4 billion	Recipient $194.3 million
Brazil	$1.057 trillion	$ 6,150	5%	7.5%	$46.9 billion	$48.7 billion	Recipient $1.012 billion
Canada	$722.3 billion	$23,300	1.7%	7.6%	$277 billion	$259.3 billion	Donor $2.1 billion
China	$4.8 trillion	$3,800	-1.3%	10%	$194.9 billion	$165.8 billion	Not Available
Colombia	$245.1 billion	$6,200	9.2%	20%	$11.5 billion	$10 billion	Recipient $40.7 million
Cuba	$18.6 billion	$1,700	0.3%	6%	$1.4 billion	$3.2 billion	Recipient $68.2 million
France	$1.373 trillion	$23,300	0.5%	11%	$304.7 billion	$280.8 billion	Donor $6.3 billion
Hong Kong	$158.2 billion	$23,100	-4%	6%	$169.98 billion	$174.4 billion	none
Israel	$105.4 billion	$18,300	1.3%	9.1%	$23.5 billion	$30.6 billion	Recipient $1.1 billion
Japan	$2.95 trillion	$23,400	-0.8%	4.7%	$413 billion	$306 billion	Donor $9.1 billion
Luxembourg	$14.7 billion	$34,200	1.1%	2.7%	$7.5 billion	$9.6 billion	Donor $160 million
Mexico	$865.5 billion	$8,500	15%	2.5%	$142.1 billion	$136.8 billion	Recipient $1.16 billion
Russia	$620.3 billion	$4,200	86%	12.4%	$75.4 billion	$48.2 billion	Recipient $8.523 billion
South Africa	$296.1 billion	$6,900	5.5%	30%	$28 billion	$26 billion	Recipient $676.3 million
Sierra Leone	$2.5 billion	$500	30%	Not available	$41 million	$166 million	Recipient $203.7 million
Turkey	$409.4 billion	$6,200	65%	7.3%	$26 billion	$40 billion	Recipient $195 million
United Kingdom	$1.29 trillion	$21,800	2.3%	6%	$271 billion	$305.9 billion	Donor $3.4 billion
United States	$9.255 trillion	$33,900	2.3%	4.2%	$663 billion	$912 billion	Donor $6.9 billion

Figures from CIA World Factbook, 2000.

Pay attention!

Use with page 49.

Name _____

Use the information from page 48 to answer the questions below.

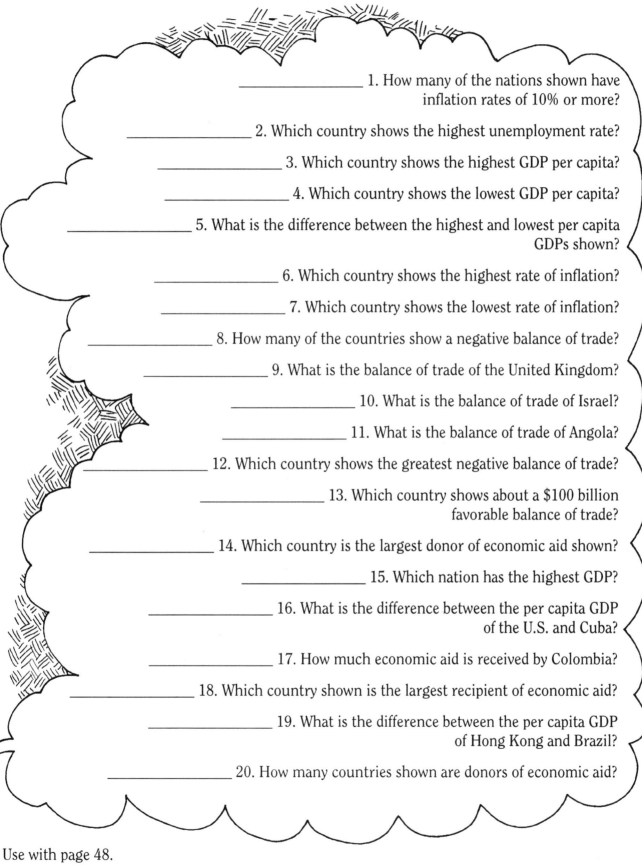

_____ 1. How many of the nations shown have inflation rates of 10% or more?

_____ 2. Which country shows the highest unemployment rate?

_____ 3. Which country shows the highest GDP per capita?

_____ 4. Which country shows the lowest GDP per capita?

_____ 5. What is the difference between the highest and lowest per capita GDPs shown?

_____ 6. Which country shows the highest rate of inflation?

_____ 7. Which country shows the lowest rate of inflation?

_____ 8. How many of the countries show a negative balance of trade?

_____ 9. What is the balance of trade of the United Kingdom?

_____ 10. What is the balance of trade of Israel?

_____ 11. What is the balance of trade of Angola?

_____ 12. Which country shows the greatest negative balance of trade?

_____ 13. Which country shows about a $100 billion favorable balance of trade?

_____ 14. Which country is the largest donor of economic aid shown?

_____ 15. Which nation has the highest GDP?

_____ 16. What is the difference between the per capita GDP of the U.S. and Cuba?

_____ 17. How much economic aid is received by Colombia?

_____ 18. Which country shown is the largest recipient of economic aid?

_____ 19. What is the difference between the per capita GDP of Hong Kong and Brazil?

_____ 20. How many countries shown are donors of economic aid?

Use with page 48.

Name

NEWSWORTHY EVENTS

The friendly banker, Mr. Bigg de Posit, likes to end each day surrounded by a big batch of daily newspapers to read. With his sharp eyes and financially-inclined mind, he notices that these headlines are all connected to the economy. Scrutinize each headline and decide what economic concept is connected to it.

1. MEGA-SALES SPUR EARLY HOLIDAY SHOPPING

2. UNEMPLOYMENT RISES AS ECONOMY SLOWS

3. Diamond Imports Heavily Taxed

4. Sunshine Airways Lowers Prices; Other Carriers Follow

5. DEEP ECONOMIC TROUBLES FOLLOW STOCK MARKET CRASH

6. RECESSION IN ASIA SLOWS U.S. INVESTMENTS

7. CITY OUTGROWS ITS WATER SUPPLY

8. Nurse Shortage Leads to Higher Salaries

9. GOVERNMENT EXPANDS FOOD-STAMP PROGRAM

10. Giant Phone Companies Merge; Drive Small Companies Out of Business

11. Purchasing Power Increases for Average Citizen

12. NORTHWEST TRUCKERS STRIKE; SHIPMENTS AT STANDSTILL

Write the number of the headline that is related to . . .

_____ A. recession

_____ B. the concept of scarcity

_____ C. tariffs

_____ D. the law of supply and demand

_____ E. the Great Depression

_____ F. a nation's GDP per capita

_____ G. competition

_____ H. global economy

_____ I. monopoly

_____ J. distribution

_____ K. welfare

_____ L. incentives

Name _____

50

APPENDIX

CONTENTS

TERMS FOR ECONOMICS

alloy — a mixture of two or more metals (often used to make coins)

ATM — (automated teller machine) a machine that performs banking operations

ATM card — a bankcard that allows customers to complete transactions at an automatic teller machine

balance — the amount of money in a bank account

balance of payments — a statement of all the goods, services, and money payments that flow in and out of a country in a given period; the difference between the amount of foreign currency a country takes in and the amount it spends in foreign currency

balance of trade — the difference between the value of a country's imports and exports

balanced budget — a budget in which the money taken in is equal to or greater than the amount of money going out

bank statement — a written monthly summary of a customer's bank transactions

bear market — a period during which the stock market is not doing well, and the stock prices go down

bills of credit — the first currency, issued by the colony of Massachusetts

bond — a certificate of a loan to a business or government

boom — a period of rapid economic growth

bounced check — a check that is returned by the bank because of lack of funds

budget — a plan of how much money is able to be spent and how it will be spent

bull market — a period during which the stock market is doing well, and the stock prices go up

business — a venture that brings in money from selling goods or services

capital — money used to buy things used in a business; also non-money things such as equipment, that can be used to produce goods

capitalism — an economic system in which most of the ownership of the companies producing goods and services is held by private individuals

cashier's check — a check that is guaranteed by a bank

check — a written order for a bank to pay an amount of money to a person or business from money in a bank account

circulation — money that is available for use

clearinghouse — a place where banks handle accounts and exchange checks

collateral — property that a borrower promises to give to a lender if the borrower cannot pay a loan

competition — more than one business selling the same product (or similar products)

consumer — someone who buys and/or uses goods and services

continentals — the paper money printed by the U.S. Congress during the American Revolutionary War

corporation — a business organization that is owned by a number of people known as stockholders

cosign — to sign a loan for another person, taking responsibility if the other person defaults

cost of living — the cost of buying goods and services that are needed for daily living

counterfeit — a "fake" copy of something (such as money) that others think is real

credit — money loaned that must be paid back

credit card — a card that allows its holder to buy things on credit

credit limit — the amount of credit available to a person

credit terms — the conditions arranged at the time of credit (interest rate, length of credit, minimum payments, fees, etc.)

currency — any kind of money that is used as a medium of exchange

debit card — a bank card that allows a person to withdraw money from a checking account electronically

debt — money owed when it is borrowed or when something is bought on credit

demand — the desire of consumers for a product or service

denomination — the value of a particular bill or coin

deposit — money put into an account

depression — an extended period of slump in business activity

distribution — the process by which goods and services are spread out among customers

dividend — a share of profits received by a stockholder

donate — to contribute money, time, or goods to a worthy cause or charity

DOW — (Dow Jones Industrial Average) a number that represents the average closing prices of 30 selected stocks

down payment — a lump sum of money paid as the first payment on a debt

eagle — an early gold coin made in the U.S.

earned income — money someone receives from working

economy — the way that resources are used in a society to produce and distribute goods and services

endorse — to sign the back of a check

entrepreneur — someone who creates and manages a business

exchange rate — the value of one nation's currency expressed in terms of another nation's currency

exports — the goods that are sent from one country to be sold in other countries

FDIC — (Federal Deposit Insurance Corporation) government organization that insures deposits in most U.S. banks

FTC — (Federal Trade Commission) U.S. agency that works to maintain fare competition in the economy and protect consumers from unfair economic practices

Federal Reserve System — (FRS) the United States' central banking system

gold standard — a system of currency in which the money can be exchanged for an amount of gold

greenbacks — the first official paper money printed by the United States government

goods — real items that can be bought or sold

GDP — (Gross Domestic Product) the value of all the goods and services produced in a country during a given period of time, including those produced by companies that are foreign-owned

GNP — (Gross National Product) the value of all the goods and services produced by a country during a given period, including those produced outside of the country

IMF — (International Monetary Fund) organization of the U.N. that works to improve financial dealings between different countries

53

inflation — a continued increase in prices throughout an economy

ingot — metal made into a shape, such as bars, before it is shaped into something else

installment — a partial payment of a debt, paid on a regular basis

interest — the amount or rate of money paid to borrow money; the amount of money paid by a bank to its depositors

investment — the risk of money or other resource in hopes of getting something in return

laissez faire — the theory that the government should not interfere with businesses

Law of Demand — states that, in general, the price of a product increases as demand for the product increases

Law of Supply — states that, in general, the price of a product decreases as the supply of it increases

line of credit — an amount of money that a bank has agreed can be loaned to someone

loan — money borrowed for a certain amount of time

mature — to get to the point in time where the investment can be redeemed (or cashed in)

medium of exchange — anything used as a trade for goods and services

milled coin — a coin with ridges

minimum deposit — the least amount of money required to open an account

mint — a place where coins are made; to make coins

money — anything people give in exchange for goods and services

monopoly — a condition existing when there is only one business that sells a product or provides a service in a market

money order — a written order to give an amount of money to a person or business

mortgage — a loan that is given to buy property or a house

mutual fund — a company that sells stock in itself and uses the money to invest in other companies

national debt — the amount of money owed by the federal government

natural resource — anything that is found naturally on the earth

need — something that people must have

nonprofit — businesses that do not intend to make a profit

pawnshop — a business where someone can leave an item of value in exchange for a loan

PIN — (personal identification number) a code that a person uses to carry out business transactions at an ATM machine or with other accounts

principal — the amount of money in an account or on a loan, not including the interest

private sector — the part of the economy wherein things are produced or services are offered by private individuals or businesses

54

producer — the people or businesses that provide foods and services

production — the process by which goods and services are made

profit — the money a business earns above the costs of running the business

promissory note — a written promise to pay back a loan

public sector — the part of the economy wherein things are produced or services are offered by the government

recession — a period of economic slowdown, but not as severe as a depression

register — the part of a checkbook where all transactions are written

reserve — money that is kept in a bank and not available for loan

risk — the chance of a loss

safe-deposit box — a locked box at a bank that is a safe place for valuable items

salary — a fixed amount of money paid for work, usually agreed-upon at a yearly rate

sales tax — a tax added on to the price of goods and services

savings — money that someone does not spend but puts away to be used later

services — work done for people by other people

share — a part of a company that can be bought by someone as an investment

Social Security — a federal government system of support for retired workers and others who are not able to work

standard of living — the economic level at which a nation or individual lives (the value of the goods and services consumed by the nation or individual within a period of time)

stock — a part of a company that is available to be purchased by the public

stockholder — a person who holds shares of stock in a company

stock market — a place where shares of stock of many companies are bought and sold

supply — the amount of a good or service that is available to people to purchase

surcharge — an extra cost or tax added onto the cost of something

tariff — a tax on imported or exported goods

taxes — money that a government collects from people or businesses

tax-exempt — not required to pay taxes

transaction — any business done with a bank

traveler's check — a special check used instead of cash, issued by a bank

unearned income — money earned from sources other than work (such as investments or interest)

unemployment — being out of work

wages — money paid to an employee for work done, often paid at an hourly rate

Wall Street — a New York City street where major companies do business; a symbol of the U.S. financial world

want — something that someone would like to have but does not necessarily need

warranty — a written guarantee that comes with the purchase of some products to replace or repair the product if something goes wrong

welfare — income paid by the government to people who need assistance to live

withdrawal — money taken from a bank account

Another little dividend!

Coo!

ECONOMICS SKILLS TEST

> Gilbert has money to invest —
> $5000 to be exact.

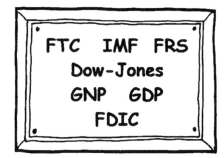

1. If he puts it in a savings account at 4.5% interest, how much will it be worth at the end of a year?_____

2. If he buys 200 shares of a stock at $25 a share, and the share increases to $33 a share, how much will it be worth if he sells at $33?_____

3. If he buys a 12-month CD at 6.2% interest, how much will it be worth at the end of the year?_____

4–10: Circle the correct answer.

4. Cal has made a deposit into a new bank account which requires him to leave the money for 1 year in order to get the rate of interest promised. What kind of account is this?
   a. a CD
   b. an ATM
   c. a checking account
   d. a savings account

5. Bill has an IRA at his local bank. The reason for this account is probably
   a. to pay off college loans.
   b. to pay for an new automobile.
   c. to save for retirement.
   d. to pay for a safe-deposit box.

6. Moe is using his ATM card. Which of the following is he probably NOT doing?
   a. making a deposit in his account
   b. opening a new account
   c. making a withdrawal from his account
   d. making a loan payment

7. Moe is leaving his good CD player at a place in exchange for a quick loan at high interest rates. He is probably visiting
   a. a bank.   c. a stockbroker.
   b. a credit union. d. a pawnshop.

8. Penny is paid an hourly rate of $11 for her job as a cashier. This money is called
   a. a salary.   c. her wages.
   b. a bonus.   d. interest.

9. Wanda puts some money into a new company, hoping to make a profit. She takes a risk that she will lose some or all of the money. This money is
   a. a donation.   c. a money order.
   b. an investment.   d. savings.

10. After Cassius pays all his living expenses from the money he has earned, he has some money left over to save or spend on a vacation. This extra money is called
    a. benefits.   c. unearned income.
    b. interest.   d. disposable income.

11–14: Write an answer chosen from the sign.

```
FTC   IMF   FRS
   Dow-Jones
  GNP    GDP
     FDIC
```

11. Which insures bank deposits? _____

12. Which tells something about the condition of the U.S. stock market? _____

13. Which measures the purchasing power (value of goods & services) of a nation? _____

14. Which assists with financial dealings between countries? _____

Name _____

15–24: Write or choose the correct answer.

15. Where are U.S. coins made? _____

16. Of what material are U.S. coins made? _____

17. What is one of the sayings on all U.S. coins? _____

18. Where is U.S. paper currency made? _____

19. What is the largest U.S. bill in circulation? _____

20. What is meant by a gold standard? _____

21. Lottie has six U.S. coins totaling 66¢. What is the value of her milled coins? _____

22. Tell two ways that U.S. bills are made with safeguards against counterfeiting:

    _____

    _____

23. Penny bought a 6-month CD for $2000 with 5% annual interest. Her friend Lester put $2400 in a savings account at 4% annual interest. They both withdrew all the money at the end of 6 months. Who withdrew the most money? _____

24. Moe purchased a bike with a credit card. The interest rate on the card is 18%. The bike cost $450. Mike paid $50 a month, so that the cost of the bike and the interest were all paid by the end of the year. About how much did he pay for the bike?
    a. $460   b. $500   c. $575   d. $650

25–34: Find a term on the sign to complete each sentence. Write the letter on the line.

25. Elmer keeps track of checking account transactions by writing them in his check _____.

26. B.J. bought a new car because he wanted the protection that comes with the five-year_____.

27. Mr. dePosit cannot spend his collection of greenbacks because they are out of _____.

28. To slow down inflation, the Federal Reserve requires its banks to keep more money in _____.

29. Brenda has bought a _____, which is a certificate of a loan to a business or government.

30. The _____ is the amount Penny owes on her loan, not including interest.

31. Stockholders are happy with a _____ market.

32. A 15%_____ was added to Theodora's hotel bill.

33. R.D. must make a payment every month, or he will _____ on his bank loan.

34. To deposit a check, Theodora must _____ the back of the check.

a. warranty	k. alloy
b. stock	l. bond
c. ingot	m. circulation
d. bear	n. principal
e. default	o. bull
f. debt	p. profit
g. currency	q. milled
h. endorse	r. mortgage
i. reserve	s. register
j. share	t. surcharge

Name _____

35–36: Use the information from this ad to answer the questions. Write the answer on the line.

35. Bill Bucks enjoyed one of these tropical vacations. He and his wife stayed 6 days. How much did they pay for their trip?

_____

ENJOY A TROPICAL VACATION
PARADISE ISLAND
$160 A DAY PER PERSON
INCLUDES
FOOD, AIRFARE, HOTEL, RECREATION
CALL PARADISE TRAVEL
555-1555
Additional 6% state tax and 10% hotel surcharge

36. Moe Monnie took two friends on a trip to Paradise Island. They stayed for 4 days. Moe put the whole trip on his credit card, which charges 12% interest. He paid the whole amount and the interest after 6 months. How much did he pay? _____

37–40: Circle or write one or more answers for each question.

37. Lenny and his friends started a lemonade stand. Soon the weather turned very hot, and demand for lemonade soared. They could hardly keep up with the orders. Which of these probably happened?
   a. They started to make a profit.
   b. They raised their prices.
   c. They lowered their prices.
   d. They started to make more lemonade.

38. All of a sudden, the weather turned cold and rainy. Very few customers wanted lemonade. Which ideas would be wise?
   a. Increase lemonade production.
   b. Decrease lemonade production.
   c. Lower prices.
   d. Raise prices.

39. A neighbor started a lemonade stand down the street from Lenny's. Some of his customers bought from the neighbor. What will Lenny probably do?
   a. Lower prices.
   b. Raise prices.
   c. Increase lemonade production.
   d. Decrease lemonade production.

40. What are some other things Lenny might do to keep his customers?

   _____

   _____

   _____

41–44: Use Penny's bank book to answer the questions. Write the correct answers on the lines.

_____ 41. What interest rate does her account give?

_____ 42. What was her balance on 7-17-01?

_____ 43. How much was withdrawn on 9-12-01?

_____ 44. What was her balance on 10–26-01?

SAVINGS ACCOUNT # 407-001

Date	Deposits	Withdrawals	Interest	Balance
1/1/00				350.00
12/31/00			14.00	364.00
7/15/01	66.00			
9/12/01				400.00
10/26/01		216.00		

Name

45–50: Write the answer to each question.

Cassius Currency had a 2-week vacation from work. He had two vacation choices. He could choose the low-cost camping vacation. He would drive to a national park, sleep in a tent, enjoy the outdoors, and cook his own food over the camp stove. He would have to spend about 4 days driving, and spend about $150 for food and gas. His other choice was a luxury trip to Hawaii. He could fly there, stay in a hotel, eat, and enjoy recreational activities for $1100 a week. Cassius chose the Hawaii trip.

45. What are the benefits of this choice? _____

_____

_____

46. What are the consequences (costs)? _____

_____

_____

Joe has been saving money for four years to go to college. He has just enough money in his account to allow him to get started. The rest of the money he needs, he can earn while he attends college and during the summers. Then a friend offers him a good deal on a car. The car is almost new, and it is really a hot car! He can buy it if he takes a third of his college money. Joe really wants this car.

47. What are the positive incentives for Joe to buy the car? _____

_____

_____

48. What are the negative incentives for Joe to buy the car? _____

_____

_____

49. Circle the letters of the true statements.
   A. A developed nation has a low GDP.
   B. The UN provides economic aid to countries.
   C. Non-profit organizations are tax-exempt.
   D. The IRS regulates trade among nations.

50. Circle the letters of the true statements.
   A. Welfare provides income to people in need.
   B. Medicare provides tax-relief for citizens.
   C. A nation with a balance-of-payments surplus is likely to have currency with a declining exchange rate.

Items 51–55. Each of the headlines is related to one of the economic events or concepts shown in the list. Write the correct letter to match each headline.

A. inflation
B. recession
C. depression
D. free enterprise system
E. foreign economic aid
F. unemployment
G. a nation's GNP
H. a socialistic economy
I. availability of money
J. a nation's balance of trade
K. a nation's balance of payments
L. foreign exchange rate of currency

_____ 51.   _____ 52.   _____ 53.   _____ 54.   _____ 55.

51. **NATION'S EXPORTS EXCEED IMPORTS BY $72 MILLION**

52. **Economic Boom Sends Prices Soaring**

53. **FED LOWERS RESERVE REQUIREMENT**

54. **CANADIAN DOLLAR FALLS TO 61.5% OF U.S. DOLLAR**

55. **Government Controls 90% of All Businesses**

SCORE: Total Points _____ out of a possible 100 points

Name

ECONOMICS
SKILLS TEST ANSWER KEY

1. $5225
2. $6600
3. $5310
4. a
5. c
6. b
7. d
8. c
9. b
10. d
11. FDIC
12. Dow-Jones
13. GNP or GDP
14. IMF
15. U.S. mints (Philadelphia and Denver)
16. alloy of copper and nickel
17. *E Pluribus Unum*
    or *In God We Trust*
18. U.S. Bureau of Engraving & Printing
    (Washington D.C.)
19. $100
20. currency is backed by gold
21. 50¢
22. Answers will vary; some possibilities
    are: security thread, watermark,
    special inks, microprinting
23. Lester
24. b
25. s
26. a
27. m
28. i
29. l

30. n
31. o
32. t
33. e
34. h
35. $2227.20 (Accept answer that is
    close to this amount.)
36. $2360.83 (Accept answer that is
    close to this amount.)
37. a and b
38. b and c
39. a and d
40. Answers will vary.
41. 4%
42. $430
43. $30
44. $184
45–48: Answers may vary somewhat; accept
    answers that give reasonable descriptions
    of benefits and consequences.
45. no driving, more time for vacation,
    food provided, luxury accommodations
46. money, loses experience of camping
47. the offer made by a friend—good deal;
    prestige of hot car
48. loss of college money
49. B and C
50. A
51. J
52. A
53. I or B
54. L
55. H

ANSWERS

pages 10–11

1. yes	21. no
2. yes	22. no
3. no	23. no
4. yes	24. yes
5. yes	25. yes
6. no	26. no
7. yes	27. no
8. no	28. yes
9. no	29. yes
10. yes	30. yes
11. no	31. no
12. yes	32. no
13. no	33. yes
14. no	34. no
15. no	35. no
16. no	36. yes
17. yes	37. yes
18. yes	38. yes
19. yes	39. yes
20. yes	40. no

pages 12–13

1. b, c
2. d
3. a
4. a, b, c, d
5. a, c
6. c
7. b
8. d
9. c
10. a, c
11. a
12. b
13. a, b
14. a, d
15. c
16. a
17. d
18. c
19. d
20. d
21. d
22. d

pages 14–15

1. eagles
2. $10—eagle $5—half eagle $2.50—quarter eagle
3. U.S. mints
4. Denver and Philadelphia
5. alloys of copper and nickel
6. tiny letter on front of coin
7. ingots
8. ridges
9. dime and quarter
10. San Francisco or New Orleans
11. "In God We Trust"
12. "E Pluribus Unum"
13. "Out of many, one"

page 16

1. bills of credit (Massachusetts)
2. continentals
3. dollar (or Federal Reserve Notes)
4. Bureau of Engraving & Printing
5. Washington, D.C.
6. cotton & linen
7. $100
8. Answers may vary depending upon how much research students do. These are some of the outstanding security features: security thread, microprinting, watermark, color-shifting inks
9. destroyed or shredded-taken out of circulation
10. 18 months
11. A. $1—George Washington
    B. $5—Abraham Lincoln
    C. $10—Alexander Hamilton
    D. $20—Andrew Jackson
    E. $50—Ulysses S. Grant
    F. $100—Benjamin Franklin

page 17

1. serial number; each bill has its own number to identify the bill
2. U.S. Secretary of the Treasury
3. date the bill was first put into circulation
4. location of the Federal Reserve Bank that issued the bill
5. the Great Seal
6. watchful eye of God over the nation
7. symbol of the U.S.-stands for strength
8. stands for the first 13 states
9. the denomination of the bill
10. A. "He has favored our undertakings"
    B. "new order of the ages"

page 18

1. income
2. employee
3. benefits or bonuses
4. employer
5. producers
6. minimum wage
7. salary
8. interest
9. investment
10. wage

page 19

1. advertising
2. is correct
3. donation
4. disposable income or profit
5. is correct
6. loan, or credit
7. interest
8. budget
9. check, cash, money order, or credit card
10. wants

Basic Skills/Economics 6-8+

pages 20–21

1. $1960
2. a
3. $18
4. a
5. $29,300
6. $60
7. $4280, or $4480 is all hours over 160 are counted as overtime
8. approximately $870
9. carpenter

pages 22–23

A.	8-A
B.	4-A
C.	20-A
D.	25-D
E.	30-A
F.	1-A
G.	24-A
H.	10-A
I.	7-A
J.	19-A
K.	15-D
L.	2-D
M.	18-A
N.	21-D
O.	11-D
P.	14-D
Q.	6-D
R.	16-A
S.	5-A
T.	17-D
U.	12-D
V.	23-D
W.	29-D
X.	26-A
Y.	13-A
Z.	3-D
AA.	27-A
BB.	22-A
CC.	9-D
DD.	17-A
EE.	28-D
FF.	1-D
GG.	32-A
HH.	31-A

pages 24–25

1. 5%
2. withdrawal of $634.50
3. deposit of $1420.00
4. $2348.03
5. $2262.13
6. $2294.16
7. b
8. $763.12 or $763.13
9. Cassius
10. yes
11. 92
12. $1843.14
13. Cassius
14. $75

pages 26–27

1. $96.97
2. $16.10
3. $150.00
4. $43.77
5. $16.55
6. b
7. c
8. twice
9. the number of the check
10. the routing number (identifies the bank's Federal Reserve district), the bank number, the bank account number, and the check number
11. signed his name on the back
12. He wrote a check for more money than he had.
13. The bank sent the check back without paying it to the shop.
14. A check that works like cash; a safe way to carry checks-people pay a fee for the checks; they are replaced if lost
15. a check you purchase from a bank, guaranteed by the bank

pages 28–29

1. E
2. N
3. F
4. M
5. J
6. A
7. I
8. C
9. D
10. O
11. H
12. L
13. P
14. G
15. K
16. B

pages 30–31

1. R
2. Q
3. G
4. B
5. J
6. A
7. C

pages 32–33

The budgets will vary. Check to make sure that the student creates a budget which will work—one that has incoming money equal to or exceeding the money going out.

1–2. Look for suggestions that are reasonable, sound advice for budgeting.

pages 34–35

Student conclusions about benefits and consequences will vary. Those listed below are possible answers:
1. benefits: she keeps some of her money, gets a nice jacket; consequences: she gets less quality and style than the $398 jacket, spends more money than if she'd bought the $88 jacket
2. benefits: he sets his own schedule, doesn't have a difficult split schedule; consequences: less money, no insurance

3. benefits: she saved money, she had a car when she got to Nashville; consequences: lost time, wear and tear on her car
4. benefits: good feelings, helping someone; consequences: gave up health club membership
5. benefits: saved time, gained independence, didn't have to ride the bus; consequences: has to work, gains financial responsibilities
6. benefits: doesn't have to cook, gets better food; consequences: spends more money on food
7. benefits: saved money; consequences: loss of prestige, doesn't have a great-looking bike, less speed, no warranty

pages 36–37

1. $420
2. yes
3. yes
4. no
5. yes
6. $564
7. yes
8. Answers will vary.

pages 38–39

Correct answers (that should be circled) are:
1, 8, 9, 11, 12, 14, 18, 19, 21

pages 40–41

Student conclusions may vary on these items. Allow answers that students can explain, using understandings about supply & demand, prices, and competition. Answers that Elmer has correctly chosen are: 1, 4, 6.

pages 42–43

Answers may vary on these items. The answers given below are possibilities.
1. interest rate at bank
2. sale on skateboards, peer pressure
3. sale price, possibility of having flashy new skateboard
4. giving up the money (most of his gift), peer pressure
5. avoiding borrowing money and paying interest
6. unreliability of car, costs of fixing old car, embarrassment
7. possibility of profit
8. possibility of losing his investment, fear of fashion change, uneasiness about Lenny's history with financial deals
9. possibility of making money
10. possibility of losing money
11. good feelings, ability to help the child
12. missing the concert and the fun trip

pages 44–45

1. Answers will vary. Check to see that student has listed at least 5 things that are actually paid for with tax dollars.
2. $615.75
3. $71.00
4. $450.34
5. $14,220
6. D
7. G
8. E
9. I
10. J
11. K
12. L
13. H

14. B
15. C
16. A
17. F
18. M

pages 46–47

1. Federal Reserve System
2. monetary
3. the Board of Governors; U.S. president; 14 years
4. Federal Open Market Committee
5. money it raises from investments and fees
6. Congress
7. 12
8. interest
9. raise
10. lower
11. inflation
12. a) more
    b) lower
    c) lower
    d) easier
13–24. The following numbers should be circled to show correct statements:
    14, 16, 17, 18, 22

pages 48–49

1. 6
2. South Africa (angola is also acceptable)
3. Luxembourg
4. Sierra Leone
5. $33,700
6. Belarus
7. Hong Kong
8. 11
9. –$34.9 billion (unfavorable balance)
10. –$7.1 billion (unfavorable balance)
11. +$2 billion (favorable balance)
12. U.S.
13. Japan
14. Japan
15. U.S.
16. $32,200
17. $40.7 million
18. Russia
19. $16,950
20. 7

page 50

A.	2
B.	7
C.	3
D.	8
E.	5
F.	11
G.	4
H.	6
I.	10
J.	12
K.	9
L.	1